EFFECTIVE SCHEDULING

If you are always late or in a hurry, it is probably a sign that your time could be better managed.

THE SCHOOL-TO-WORK LIBRARY

EFFECTIVE SCHEDULING

Sue Hurwitz

GLOBE FEARON EDUCATIONAL PUBLISHER
A Division of Simon & Schuster
Upper Saddle River, New Jersey

To our granddaughter, Adina

Published in 1996 by The Rosen Publishing Group, Inc.
29 East 21st Street, New York, NY 10010

First Edition

Printed in the United States of America

ISBN 0-835-91794-0

Contents

Effective scheduling can help you to plan ahead in the short term and long term.

Introduction

WHAT IS EFFECTIVE SCHEDULING? WHY IS IT important to achieve?

Effective scheduling is using time to your best advantage. When you schedule your time effectively, you accomplish more during a certain period of time. The more you get done, the higher your performance rate.

How do you know if your scheduling is effective?

Are you able to do everything you need to do and still have time to do the things you like to do? For example, after you finish your homework, do you still have time for other activities?

After you participate in activities, do you have time to do your homework? When you are early, do you use that time to think about solutions to your problems? Are you able to refuse to do something you would like to do because there are other things you need to do?

If you answer no to any of the above questions, your scheduling probably is not as effective as it could be. If your scheduling becomes more effective, you will have more time to do the things you want to do.

In addition, greater demands will be placed on your time as you get older. You will be better prepared to meet these demands if you know how to schedule your time effectively.

The Challenge of a Changing World

As the year 2000 approaches, North Americans find themselves living more and more in a worldwide economy. We have access to information and ideas that were unknown a mere twenty-five years ago. But this increased knowledge takes time to gather and time to organize.

We need time to learn how to use knowledge to our best advantage. We need time to learn new skills to succeed and to adapt to a changing world with changing roles and expectations.

Yet we find that our precious resource of time is still only twenty-four hours each day. Time is a limited resource that cannot be replaced once it is used. And it must be used the moment we get it. We must learn to schedule it wisely, but that is often easier said than done.

You may often find yourself saying "I don't have enough time for that" or wondering why other people are able to get more done. Sometimes it is

simply a matter of figuring out how to organize
yourself—and your time—better.

This book looks at ways to help improve the
scheduling of your time. It discusses ways to meet
deadlines. It suggests timesaving techniques to use
at school, at work, and in your future career. These
techniques and habits can help you become the
kind of person you want to be.

Effective scheduling can make your life simpler
and more pleasant. It can help you use your time
wisely. Learning to use effective scheduling can lead
to higher performance now and in the future. Effective scheduling skills can give you a competitive
edge in the high-performance workplace of the new
century.

Planning, or scheduling, how you spend your
time can help you bring your time under control
and use it better. You can choose how you will
spend your time. Once you have your time effectively scheduled, you have your life under control—
which means that you will be able to do more of the
things you have to do and more of the things you
want to do.

As a student, you have many demands on your time.

Scheduling at School

WE ALL HAVE THE SAME LIMITED AMOUNT OF time: sixty seconds in each minute, sixty minutes in each hour. Time cannot be saved; we must use it immediately. We cannot control the time we have, but we *can* control how we use it. That is why scheduling is important.

Many demands are placed on your time at school. You must get to class—on time. You must turn in your assignments—on time. You must get to after-school activities—on time. You must study and complete homework—on time.

Sometimes the demands placed on your time may seem overwhelming. How can you get everything done? How do other students manage? How do you start? Where do you start?

Learning effective scheduling techniques can help you deal with these questions. The best time to start is now. What tasks, or things, do you need to do today and tonight? These are your short-term goals.

What tasks do you want to accomplish during the

next week, or the next month, or next year? These are long-term goals.

Lists

Lists are tools to help you remember things. A list may also be used to help you decide how to schedule your time.

When you make a list it is more effective to cluster tasks, or schedule similar tasks together. For instance, suppose you need to return something to the school library. You also need to stop by your locker, which is down the same hallway. If you cluster these tasks by making one trip to do them both, you schedule your time to your advantage.

Short-Term Goals

A good way of identifying tasks is to write out a list of everything you must do. To start your list, identify the things you must do in the next day or so.

Put tasks that are not urgent at the bottom of the list. Tasks that are not necessary should be eliminated altogether. When your list is completed, the tasks at the top of your list are your priority tasks—the most important and the ones to focus on first.

Next, rank your priority list in order, putting the most urgent tasks at the top of the new list. Suppose you need to study for tomorrow's math quiz, call your friend, go to the library to do research for

By using your time effectively, you can approach tests and exams with confidence instead of panic.

a term paper due in three weeks, and finish reading a chapter for English.

To rank those items you would put the most urgent task first, the second most important task second, and so on. On a priority list the four tasks would be listed as follows:

- Study for tomorrow's math quiz.
- Finish reading chapter for English.
- Go to library to do research for paper due in three weeks.
- Call your friend (not an urgent task, but one you might enjoy if you have time).

Always schedule at least an hour each day for yourself. Use this time for relaxing, to put some balance in your schedule. Then you can do your priority tasks better. Do whatever you want—talk on the phone, daydream, or take a TV break—while you take your mind off your tasks. If you decide to use your special time to call your friend, you needn't feel guilty because the time is in your schedule.

Making a Schedule

Once you have identified the important tasks on your priority list, the next step is to develop an effective schedule. There are several ways to make a schedule.

A teacher or counselor can help you start to plan for long-term goals.

One way is to give a certain amount of time to each task on your priority list. For instance, suppose you have from 7 p.m. to 11 p.m. to do everything on your priority list.

After looking over your list you decide to spend two hours studying for tomorrow's math quiz; an hour and a half reading your English homework; and one hour organizing your materials for your term paper. Then you will talk with your friend for half an hour.

But as you evaluate this schedule you see something wrong. You have scheduled more tasks than you have scheduled time. That won't work. The schedule must be adjusted to be effective.

Making a list of assignments or tasks can make your workload seem less overwhelming.

Thinking further, you realize that two hours to study for the math quiz probably isn't enough. You haven't done your math assignments very thoroughly for the past month, and you know you need more time to prepare for the quiz.

It would be more effective to look at the tasks and estimate how much time you think each task should take. Then schedule your time accordingly, even if it means working from 6 p.m. until midnight to get everything done.

Using this example, for instance, look over the math and estimate how much you will need to study each part of the material. Do the same with the English chapter and the research paper. Obviously, you won't be able to finish the entire research paper in one night. Which brings us to longer-term goals.

Longer-Term Goals

The priority list that we discussed for short-term goals is really a "to do" list. Longer-term tasks should be scheduled on a calendar.

A pocket notebook or assignment notebook is a good way to keep track of your "to do" list. It can also remind you of tasks to transfer to a weekly or monthly calendar.

An important thing to remember about lists and calendars is that they are scheduling tools. Lists are starting points for defining tasks, ranking tasks in order of importance, and clustering tasks. Calendars help to develop longer-term goals and to keep track of longer-term tasks.

Using a calendar, first enter the deadline of the research paper. Then work backward from the deadline, breaking the research into small steps. These small steps can be scheduled day by day to meet the deadline.

Budgeting Your Time

Scheduling your time is much like budgeting your money. In fact, someone has probably asked you the question "How did you *spend* your time today?" Or maybe you have heard the expression "Time is *money*." In fact, you can use simple money budgeting steps as another way to help you schedule your time.

The first thing to do is to set your goals. Decide what things you want to spend time on. Determine both long- and short-term goals.

Next, remember that you have twenty-four hours each day to do everything you *want* to do and everything you *have* to do, including eat, sleep, and go to school.

Next, figure out what things you *have to* spend time on every day. For example, you must spend a certain amount of hours sleeping each day. You also have to go to school five days a week and do your homework almost every day.

Then, take the total number of hours that you will spend each day doing necessary things and subtract that number from the total hours of the day—twenty-four. The number of hours you are left with is the number of hours you will have to do the things you want to do. You can then spend that time any way you please, whether you want to join a club, play sports, or just read a good book.

Let's say, for instance, that you sleep eight hours each night. And on an average weekday, you spend about eight hours at school and about two hours eating meals, getting prepared, and traveling to and from school. How much time would you have on a weekday to be part of student government, work at a part-time job, or play on the basketball team? Here's how you would figure it out:

Hours in the Day	**24**
minus	
Hours Spent Doing Necessary Activities	
Sleeping	−8
Eating, traveling, etc.	−2
School	−8
Total	−18
Hours Left for Homework, Activities and Free Time	**6**

Once you see how much time it takes you to do all the things you must do, you may find it is necessary to change your schedule. Figuring out the demands on your time is an excellent first step in effective scheduling.

Brainstorming

Brainstorming means breaking down your goals into smaller parts by listing ideas that pop freely into your mind. Brainstorming helps you look at the steps necessary to achieve your tasks. It also helps you consider possible problems you may run into on the way to achieving your tasks and to work out a backup plan.

Working backward from a deadline is a scheduling technique that will help you get your homework finished and schedule other parts of your life.

Annie

When Annie looked at her alarm clock, she saw that she had overslept nearly an hour. She jumped out of bed and slipped on her jeans and shirt. Thank goodness she'd picked out her school clothes the night before. Still, it was almost 8:00 and she had to be at the bus stop by 8:30.

As Annie washed her face and brushed her teeth, she thought about how she'd get to school on time. She had just over thirty minutes to get organized. She needed to leave the house by 8:25, she needed to be through with breakfast by 8:20, so she needed to be in the kitchen by 8:10.

Running a bit later than she had hoped, Annie got to the kitchen and popped a slice of bread into the toaster at about 8:12. She poured herself a glass of milk and swallowed her vitamin while the bread toasted. Not bothering to butter the toast, Annie grabbed it in one hand and her school books in the other hand as she rushed out the door at 8:25.

"You look stressed," Annie's friend, Shira,

commented when Annie arrived at the bus stop at 8:27.

"You might say that!" Annie answered. "Actually, I'm a bit relieved."

"Oh?" Shira asked.

"Yeah! I thought I might miss the bus and have to walk to school," Annie confessed. "I overslept this morning."

"You got here just in the nick of time," Shira pointed out. "The bus just turned the corner."

Because Annie had reviewed her morning schedule the previous evening, she knew what to do when she overslept and ran short on time. Working backward from a deadline—the scheduled arrival of the bus—she was able to adjust her activities by skipping some of her breakfast.

Annie was lucky that the bus didn't arrive early, causing her to miss it. She also was lucky that she had planned her morning routine so that she didn't panic when she saw she was running late.

Scheduling Assignments

Another good habit that will make your scheduling more effective at school is keeping track of your assignments. Many students simply write down their homework assignments on pieces of scrap paper or in different notebooks, if they write them down at

Write reminder notes to yourself about things like turning in library books on time.

all. This makes it easy to misplace or forget assignments. Try to keep a list of all your assignments in the same place—either in an assignment book or in the front of one particular notebook. This way you will always know where your daily assignments are. When you return home each night, check your assignment book first thing so you can decide how to prepare for the next school day.

Calvin

Calvin found that he kept forgetting to do his math assignments. When his math teacher kept him after class to ask him about his missing assignments, Calvin explained to her how he prepared for class.

He knew that he didn't have such a great memory—that's why he always tore a piece of paper out of his math notebook to write his math assignments on. He stuffed that piece of paper into his book bag with the rest of his things to do that night.

Taking his teacher's advice, Calvin bought a small assignment pad that he used only for keeping track of his homework and tests. Each day on the way home from school, he looked over what he was assigned that day so that he could set up a schedule for doing his homework that evening. Soon after he began this method, his teacher noticed that Calvin's scheduling had allowed him to complete his assignments on time. Calvin noticed that the time that he used to spend searching for his assignments could now be used to play more basketball after school. His performance in math improved thanks to the attention he paid to his assignments.

Contingency Planning

Another good scheduling technique is to make a contingency plan, or backup plan. No one can foresee every pitfall or crisis that may challenge your scheduling. Contingency planning helps to limit the negative effects of things that may go wrong.

Jeff

When the drama class needed volunteers to work on

Scheduling is often important for group projects, as group members coordinate their efforts to meet a goal.

making scenery for the spring play, Jeff was the first to sign up. Elected to be the team leader, he suggested Tuesdays and Thursdays right after school as meeting sessions for the group. The team agreed.

"We only have two months to get all the sets designed and painted," Jeff announced at the first meeting. "Since we should have the sets ready for rehearsals, that really gives us only seven weeks!"

"We will need to work more than two afternoons a week," Nancy suggested. "First, we must build the backdrops and scenery. Then we'll need to sketch and paint them. I don't think we'll have enough time in only fourteen meetings!"

"We can't use the art room any other times," Jeff explained. "We'll just have to schedule our time effectively!"

"I brought a calendar," Nancy offered. "Shall we start scheduling right now?"

"Great!" Jeff agreed. "We'll pencil in our deadline, then divide the work into seven sections. That will help us estimate what we need to get done each week. Then we'll divide each week into two sections to find out how much we need to do each time."

"What if we can't get each session's work done that day?" Nancy worried, identifying a potential problem.

"We may need to adjust our schedule and either cancel some of the scenery or ask other students to help."

"We probably could stay an extra hour sometimes if we need more time," Nancy suggested. "But we should watch our calendar so we don't get behind schedule!"

Both Jeff and Nancy used good scheduling techniques for getting the artwork done in time for the school play.

Jeff knew that sometimes it is necessary to adjust a schedule if it isn't working out. One way to adjust your schedule is to make your goals simpler so that they can be achieved more easily. Jeff also considered delegating some of the work to other students. Delegating is another good technique. No one can do *everything*!

Nancy's contingency plan was to schedule extra time if necessary. She also intended to keep an eye on their calendar to see that they didn't fall behind schedule. If they could not achieve all their goals in the allotted time, Nancy agreed that they could readjust their priorities.

These kinds of scheduling techniques can be used at school, at home, or at work. Both Jeff and Nancy were practicing important skills that made them more effective and able to accomplish their goals.

Questions to Ask Yourself

There are a lot of demands placed on you each day at school. Learning to use a schedule can improve your performance and relieve some of your stress at school. 1) What is contingency planning and how can it help your scheduling at school? 2) Is it important to include free time in your daily schedule? Why or why not? 3) What kind of short-term goals should go at the top of your priority list?

Scheduling at Work

MOST YOUNG ADULTS GIVE SOME THOUGHT TO their long-term goals. What kind of career do you want to pursue? What kind of work do you hope to be doing ten years from now? What can you do *now* to help you reach these long-term goals?

Defining long-term goals is important. Long-term goals must be worked toward in small steps: what you will do today, next week, and next month. These steps are the shorter-term goals necessary to reach your long-term goals.

The scheduling techniques of making lists and calendars are also useful at work. When you begin to juggle your school schedule and your work schedule, these effective techniques become even more helpful.

Pocket Calendar

Keep your school tasks and your work tasks on one calendar, preferably a pocket calendar. Then if your work schedule changes, you can check your calendar and reschedule your time.

Your pocket calendar can also serve as a diary to keep track of the days and hours you worked during a certain period of time. This may be an important record if problems should arise with your supervisor concerning the hours you worked.

Sometimes you may be asked to do longer-term tasks at work. Completing an inventory by next week or making out a duty-assignment list in two days are examples of longer-term tasks.

For longer-term tasks, write the deadline on your calendar. Figure out how to break the task down into smaller steps. Then work backward to schedule the smaller tasks on your calendar.

A series of small steps leading to a larger goal is called sequencing, which means working in an orderly time frame. Working on tasks in sequence can help keep you from feeling overwhelmed, or panicked, by long-range tasks.

When scheduling, it is wise to allow yourself a little extra time to meet a deadline. This cushion may help prevent a crisis when something unexpected occurs. In the workplace it is acceptable to finish a task early, but it is *rarely* acceptable to finish one late.

In making a school-work schedule, start by entering your school and work hours on your calendar. Those are the blocks of time that you work around when you schedule your study time and free time.

Carry a pocket calendar and make notes of your work schedule, especially if your hours change from week to week.

Sample School/Work Calendar							
Time	Sun.	Mon.	Tues.	Wed.	Thurs.	Fri.	Sat.
8 a.m.		class	class	class	class	class	
9 a.m.		"	"	"	"	"	work
10 a.m.		"	"	"	"	"	work
11 a.m.		"	"	"	"	"	work
12		"	"	"	"	"	work
1 p.m.		"	"	"	"	"	work
2 p.m		"	"	"	"		
3 p.m.							
4 p.m.	work		study	work	study		
5 p.m.	work		study	work	study		
6 p.m.	work		study	work	study		
7 p.m.	work			work			
8 p.m.					study		
9 p.m.			study		study		
10 p.m.			study		study		

Budgeting your time can help you avoid doing things at the last minute or at a time when you are not your most efficient.

Attitude

Your attitude can be a major asset in keeping your schedule effective both at school and at work. Learn to value your time. You will *not* be able to do everything, so become selective about tasks you agree to do. When you do select a task, stick with it until it is completed.

Learn to Say No

Learn to say no to things that distract you from focusing on your priority list. Overcommitment is stressful and frustrating. Scheduling is more

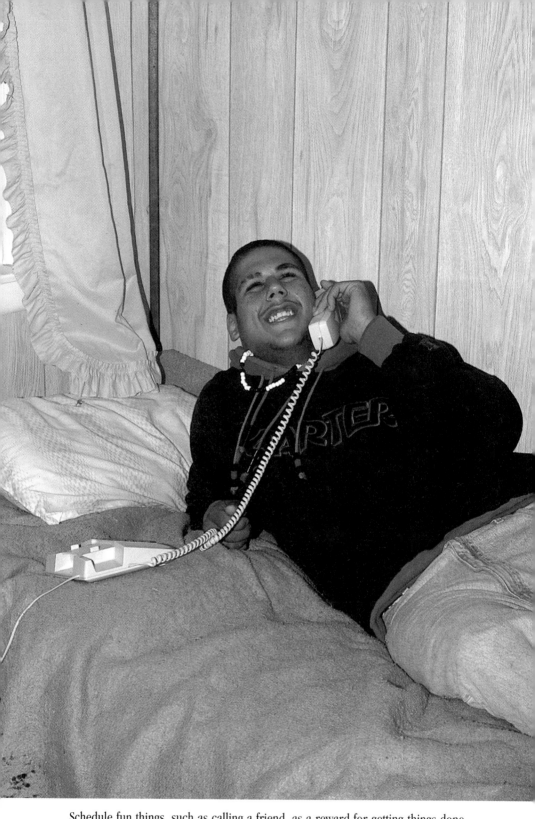

Schedule fun things, such as calling a friend, as a reward for getting things done.

effective if you do not commit to do more than you can reasonably handle along with your priority tasks.

Interruptions

Discourage telephone interruptions both at home and at school. Save them for your scheduled private time. At work, of course, never make a personal call except in an emergency.

Avoid Procrastination

Force yourself to get started by using your self-discipline. Scheduling your tasks at a certain time helps to keep you from putting tasks off. Some people procrastinate because they are afraid they cannot do a certain task.

Simplify Tasks

Think about what you don't want to do. If the task seems too difficult, break it down into smaller tasks that will be easier to accomplish. Ask yourself: What is the worst thing that can happen? When you break down the task it often does not seem so threatening.

Review and Re-evaluate Tasks

Review your schedule each night before you go to bed. Use this time to re-evaluate your day's accomplishments. Did you get your tasks done? Did you schedule more than you could do? Are there any tasks that you can cross off your list? Be proud of what you have accomplished.

Be Flexible

As you reschedule tomorrow's list, be flexible. Allow additional time if necessary for tasks that you did not finish today. If you have the time and energy, work ahead of schedule.

Be Organized

Keep your work space neat and uncluttered. A messy desk is a distraction that wastes time when you have to search for something.

Try to get off to a good start in the morning by planning the night before. Select your clothes, gather your books, or organize tasks that must be done before you leave the house. The simpler your morning routine, the more effectively you will use your time.

Time Logs

When you have trouble following your schedule, keep a time log to see how you actually spend your time. For about a week, write down how much time you spend doing each activity. Keep this notebook with you all day and record each activity as you do it.

A time log will show how effective your scheduling was, and whether or not you completed your task. For instance, if you were interrupted and didn't finish your task, write that down. If your mind wandered, write that down next to the activity you were scheduled to perform. If you were distracted by daydreaming, socializing, or talking on the phone, be sure to record that behavior.

When you review your time log, think about how you could have avoided the time wasters that got you off track. Make a note of them next to the activity. As you evaluate your time log you will see what behaviors you need to change if you really want to solve your time problems.

Tina

Tina was having trouble getting to work on time. She was almost always a minute or two late, and when she was on time, it was just minutes before she was scheduled to start working. She knew that her boss liked employees to arrive at work ten minutes early, but she rarely succeeded. She was worried that her boss was getting upset about her late arrival, though he had not said anything to her about it.

Since she had started working, Tina had also been struggling at school. The B's she was getting in some classes were not bad grades, but she was used to getting A's. Tina's parents were

Eliminating time-wasting behaviors—such as oversleeping—can help you get back on schedule.

disappointed with her grades, too, and hoped she could bring them up next term. Looking back, Tina realized she was still doing well on tests, but her homework grades were a little lower than normal.

Tina believed that her troubles at work and at school were a result of the way she used her time, but she couldn't exactly pinpoint the problem. She decided to create a time log (a record of how she spent her time) so that she could discover what the problem was. Here's what Tina found on the first day of keeping her time log:

Tina's Time Log			
Time	**Activity**	**Time Used**	**What I Did**
7:30 a.m.	Woke up	1 hr.	Got ready for school.
8:30 a.m.	School	7 hrs.	Went to classes.
3:30 p.m.	Homework	1 hr. and 25 min.	Did all math homework for tomorrow.
4:55 p.m.	Left house	10 min.	Drove to work.
5:05 p.m.	Work	3 hrs.	Had to stay an extra five minutes for coming in late.
8:05 p.m.	Left work	10 min.	Drove home.
8:15 p.m.	Free time	2 hrs.	Watched TV and talked on the phone.
10:15 p.m.	Went to bed		Slept.

While filling out her time log, Tina realized that she was trying to cram all of her studying into the block of time between school and work. As a result, she was not spending enough time on her homework assignments. This is the reason why her grades were down this past term. And because she was rushing to get all of her homework done, she was usually late for work. Before she started working, she had spent much more time on her homework. She had worked on her assignments from the time she arrived home until dinnertime.

Tina had always admired her sister Julie, who had juggled several extracurricular activities while in high school and was now working to put herself through college. Julie always seemed to organize her time well to accomplish many different things. She also managed to have time for fun. Tina asked Julie for advice on her schedule. Julie pointed out that Tina spent a lot of time talking on the phone and watching TV each night. Tina agreed that while she enjoyed this time to relax, it was taking time away from other things. Julie suggested that she give herself about an hour of relaxation time to unwind from the day. If she could get some homework done first, she could then reward herself with some TV and a few phone calls.

Tina decided to change her daily schedule in order to spend her time better. Here is what her time log looked like a week later:

Tina's Revised Time Log

Time	Activity	Time Used	What I Did
7:30 a.m.	Woke up	1 hr.	Got ready for school.
8:30 a.m.	School	7 hrs.	Went to classes.
3:30 p.m.	Homework	1 hr.	Did Geometry and English homework.
4:30 p.m.	Left house	15 min.	Drove to work.
4:45 p.m.	Work	3 hrs. and 15 min.	Boss praised me for being on time!
8:00 p.m.	Left work	10 min.	Drove home.
8:10 p.m.	Homework	50 min.	Did Biology homework and studied for French quiz.
9:00 p.m.	Free time	1 hr.	Watched TV and talked on the phone.
10:00 p.m.	Went to bed		Slept.

Tina decided to cut down on the amount of time she spent talking on the phone and watching TV. With this extra time she was able to do some of her homework before going to work and the rest when she came back home. She also had a few extra minutes for traveling time before work. Within a few weeks, Tina's time log and short-term planning helped her schedule her time more effectively. As a result, she was always early for work instead of late, and her grades went up as well.

A time log shows how you *really* spend your time. It can help you realize the need to focus on the task at hand. It can also show you how you may need to adjust your schedule: Are you always late for work because you are rushing to finish all of your homework? Do you need to reduce your "phone time"?

Ron

Ron, a senior in high school, scheduled his time effectively. He carried a full load of classes, and he worked fifteen hours a week at a restaurant. Ron had to spend his time wisely to keep up with his hectic lifestyle.

Although Ron had few activities besides school and his job, he knew that hard work was the only way he could achieve his long-term goal. He had always dreamed of going to college. He knew that

Setting deadlines is often necessary to avoid procrastination.

he needed both good grades to earn a scholarship and his wages to reach that goal.

Ron's boss, the store manager, was flexible about allowing Ron to schedule his work hours around his school exams. So during his junior year Ron experienced few scheduling problems with school and work.

Then Ron's boss resigned and a new store manager replaced him. Now, Ron began having problems. The new boss did not communicate well.

When the new boss told the employees to do something, he was not clear about deadlines. He also was not clear about who was responsible for which task. The employees began to procrastinate about doing extra tasks, hoping others would take care of them.

On one occasion the new boss asked Ron to sweep out the storage room when he had time. The restaurant was especially busy that evening. Many customers came in late after a school basketball game. Ron worked hard all evening serving customers. At closing time, he went home.

The next day, when Ron reported to work, his boss was furious because Ron hadn't cleaned up as he'd been told. Ron realized there had been a communication problem. The boss had not given Ron a deadline on cleaning the storage room, so Ron didn't make it a high priority task.

Ron explained that to his boss, then cleaned the room right away. But the extra task put him behind schedule when it came to making the inventory for reordering supplies.

As it happened, Ron had a semester test the following morning, and he did not want to stay an extra half hour to finish the inventory. So he asked his co-worker if she would finish it for him. In exchange, Ron negotiated to do one of her tasks the next afternoon.

Then Ron told his new boss that he had a previous commitment to study with a friend. He explained that he had delegated the inventory task to a co-worker. The new boss did not object as

An overload of work tasks can be a sign that you could use your time more efficiently.

long as the work was scheduled in an orderly manner.

Working conditions were not as ideal as they had been under the previous manager. But Ron kept his long-range goal in mind and readjusted his scheduling to keep his part-time job. He knew that time was on his side as long as he kept his time organized.

Jane

Jane was a junior in high school when she took a Saturday office job at a lumberyard. Jane's job was to code new products, then enter the code number into a computer.

The first Saturday Jane worked with Emily, the person she was replacing. Jane enjoyed socializing with Emily and was sorry that Emily was leaving. The following Saturday, Jane found it easy to work on her own.

But soon Jane received more and more requests for her time. Carpenters from the warehouse asked Jane to check on inventory files for them. Co-workers in the office asked her to find personnel forms for them. Sometimes she was asked to help applicants fill out forms.

Just when Jane started on her own coding tasks, she'd get another request for help. The first few Saturdays Jane didn't mind working with the other employees and doing tasks for them. She welcomed a bit of socializing. Yet she became frustrated when she ran out of time to complete her own tasks.

One Saturday, Jane was asked to take a report back to the warehouse. As she passed the lounge, she smelled coffee and donuts. She stopped to have some. Glancing at the clock, she saw it was nearly noon and she had not completed even one of her own tasks.

Jane scheduled effectively at school and at home. Yet she realized that she hadn't used good techniques in the workplace.

After several sips of coffee, Jane returned to her desk and focused on her tasks. Within five minutes, she received a request from a warehouse clerk to search for a file.

"I'll be happy to help you," Jane responded in a friendly but businesslike manner. "But I won't be able to get to it until 4:30. I have several other tasks to complete first."

About an hour later Jane was pleasantly surprised when the clerk came up to the office to search for his own file.

Jane felt good about not leaving her tasks unfinished. She also felt good about saying "no" to avoid distraction from her work in a way that did not offend her co-worker.

Questions to Ask Yourself

It can be difficult to balance your time when you have to deal with schedules at school and at work. You can use good scheduling techniques to solve such a problem. 1) What kinds of things can get in the way of your work schedule? How can you avoid them? 2) What is a time log, and how can it help you improve your daily schedule? 3) What are some steps you could take to better organize your time today?

Many employers today expect employees to be able to manage their own time and prioritize their own tasks.

Scheduling and Your Career

SCHEDULING IS VITAL IN THE WORKPLACE, JUST AS it is in a school setting. Distractions are usually greater at work and less controllable. Deadlines often have higher stakes and are less negotiable than deadlines in school.

Many workplaces are high-performance workplaces. That means that employees are expected to manage themselves and their schedules. They must set their own priorities. They must choose goal-related behaviors, habits, and ways of working that help them achieve their goals. They are responsible for completing their primary tasks. They must understand, prepare, and follow schedules. They must have enough knowledge and self-discipline to work with little or no supervision.

Communication Skills

Effective communication skills are important to use both at school and at your job. They are essential in the high-performance workplace. If you learn and practice these skills now, they will help you be better prepared for your career in the future. These skills are also time-saving devices.

Learn to be an effective listener. Pay careful attention to what your teacher or boss is saying. Ask for more information or clarification if you don't understand something. At school, practice taking notes while your teacher is talking. Later that day, look over your notes again and highlight the most important points. These notes can help you later to prepare for a test or write a paper. At work, get into the habit of carrying around a small pad of paper so that you can take notes if someone wants to discuss important data or deadlines. This will cause you to pay better attention during a conversation. After you are done, go back and highlight the key points so that you will be able to refer to them quickly and easily in the future. Write down deadlines and changes to your work schedule on your calendar.

Practice communicating your ideas effectively. Speak clearly and place emphasis on your important points. You will have more success persuading people to see your point of view if you communicate well. At work, for instance, you may need to speak with your boss. Prepare what you are going to say so that you can present your ideas in an organized manner. Your boss has limited time to listen to employees' concerns. He or she will appreciate your ability to get to the point.

Learn to read accurately and quickly. If necessary, take a course or read a "how to" book to improve your reading. Learn to speed read, paying close attention to the first and last sentences of paragraphs and the first and last paragraphs of chapters. Take notes while you read. Learn to identify important terms or phrases. By developing these communication skills, you will free up time for accomplishing other goals.

Scheduling Tools

Aside from developing good communication skills, there are some important tools you can use to help you improve your scheduling at school, work, and eventually your career. A simple example of a vital scheduling tool is a watch. By always wearing and frequently checking your watch, you can easily keep track of time. This way, you will be better prepared to meet the deadlines of your schedule.

Some other scheduling tools were also discussed in previous chapters. Priority lists, calendars, and time logs are all efficient tools in the workplace. Use them, evaluate their effectiveness, and revise them. But do not become a slave to them. Remember, they are only tools to help you accomplish your goals. You will always have more to do than you reasonably can get done. Stick to your priority goals and let the rest go until a later time.

A time log may show you areas where you can schedule your time more effectively. By identifying time wasters, you can analyze what behavior changes might get rid of the problem.

One way to make changes in your scheduling behavior is to use a problem/solution worksheet. Write down the problem and brainstorm a solution. This can help you get a clear idea of what behaviors need to be changed. Here is an example:

Problem/Solution Worksheet

Problem:	Solution:
Too many phone calls	Voice mail to screen calls

Schedule some personal quiet time in your workplace as well as at home. In the workplace, set aside 30 minutes or an hour to organize your work without interruptions. Relaxation time is important and can improve your efficiency in the long run.

Learn to delegate some of your tasks by asking someone else to take responsibility for them. Especially delegate those tasks over which you tend to procrastinate. Time does not stand still while you procrastinate, so this behavior is a huge time waster.

Think of time spent waiting as an opportunity to catch up on reading or to plan ahead.

"Want-To-Do Goals"

Priority tasks are usually "need-to" goals, tasks that we feel we must do. But there is more to life than work. We've all heard of "workaholics" who take their work so seriously that they seem not to have any fun. Psychologists warn that this is not a healthy lifestyle.

You need to put balance in your life by scheduling private time both in your personal life and in your workplace. Some people call this "mental health" time. Most of us know that even a little bit of time to call our own is a big stress-reliever.

This private time is often used for "want-to-do" goals, relaxing things that we want to do. Some people use this private time as a reward for completing their priority tasks.

You can do many things during your "want-to-do" time that will relax you and take your mind off your work. Some people like to read or write during their relaxing time. Others choose to jog or do some other type of exercise.

Long-Term "Dream" Goals

When you were younger did you dream of becoming an astronaut when you grew up? Or perhaps an artist, or a singer, or a firefighter?

As you mature you realize that a dream career requires preparation. You must get the training, the skill, or the education necessary to enable you to reach your dream.

Time spent planning and investigating long-term dream goals is well spent. These goals should be scheduled in your notebooks, calendars, and "to do" lists.

Brainstorming ideas for smaller steps that will lead to your career goal is effective scheduling. Think of your career goal as your destination. The daily, weekly, or yearly behaviors you take are the roads that eventually will lead you to your goal.

Stephen

As far back as Stephen could remember, he had

Accomplishing your school tasks more efficiently can free up time to pursue your dreams.

loved the written word. As a preschooler, picture books were his favorite pastime. In elementary school he loved to read. He spent most of his private time happily reading books, magazines, and newspapers.

By the time Stephen reached middle school, he was secretly dreaming of becoming a writer. Stephen's parents knew of his dream and encouraged him. But they also encouraged him to prepare for a job. They said that he needed to be able to earn a living while he chased his dream.

Stephen knew his parents were right, so he took classes to prepare for the workplace. But he also took classes to prepare himself for a career in writing. He enrolled in every English class offered, and he took keyboarding and computer classes. Stephen also took creative writing classes offered through the local Y.

By the time Stephen graduated from high school, he had already written many short stories. But he considered writing a hobby while he majored in computer science in college.

After graduation Stephen got a job as a programmer at a major corporation. For the next several years he worked so hard adapting to the workplace that he never found time to write. He missed it, but he was simply too tired when he got home each evening, and he had too many interruptions on the weekends.

After brainstorming for a solution to his problem, Stephen decided to get up two hours earlier every morning. He scheduled those two hours as writing time. Stephen soon found that the new schedule suited him perfectly. He was able to think more clearly during the earlier hours, and he began to pursue his dream of writing a book.

Stephen set a goal of writing two pages each morning. Some mornings when ideas flowed freely he wrote three or four pages. Some mornings when he had writer's block he wrote less than his two-page goal. But he had all the self-discipline necessary to stick to his project. And at the end of a year he had finished a book!

Stephen is now busy trying to find an agent to help him sell his book. He has started a second book while he awaits answers from agents. He is learning that writing, like any other goal, takes time to schedule and time to complete.

By working hard and using good scheduling techniques, you, like Stephen, can achieve your long- and short-term goals. Whether your career goals include going to college, going to a trade school, or finding a job when you graduate from high school, efficient scheduling will help. There is no better time than now to start scheduling. The future is right around the corner.

Questions to Ask Yourself

You can improve your chances of future success by learning scheduling techniques now. Answering these questions will help you see how to "get ahead." 1) Why are communications skills important to you at school, on the job, and in your future career? 2) What tasks do you tend to procrastinate? How can you make these tasks more manageable? 3) What are "want-to-do" goals and why are they important?

Scheduling and Your Future

HIGH PERFORMANCE THROUGH EFFECTIVE scheduling results from learning to manage your time well. Good time management can help you take charge of your time and your life. It means that you will be better able to accomplish your goals.

High performance and effective scheduling result from planning. Effective scheduling begins with defining goals, setting priorities, and using lists, calendars, and time logs.

Goals take time to consider, time to develop, and planning to achieve. When you learn and practice new behaviors to achieve your goals, you are developing your future.

Yet you should not worry so much about long-term goals that you cannot think about what you need to do today. Will I get into a certain college? Will I get that job I want? Will my grades be good enough that I can graduate from high school? All of these questions may be important. But it is impor-

You may find that you sometimes have to turn down invitations from friends in order to stick to your schedule.

tant to break long-term goals into short-term goals when you schedule your time.

Remember, yesterday is gone, tomorrow is not yet here. Any task that you perform or do not perform today will affect your tomorrows in some way. So if you want to take charge of your life, take charge of your time. Time is when things happen.

Time management is really self-management. Self-management involves habits. Ninety-five percent of all our actions are the result of habits. Effective scheduling behaviors are important in your schoolwork and in the worldwide economy. Successful people know how to schedule time effectively. With practice, you can, too!

Realize that you control how you spend your precious resource of time. Adjust your attitude and habits to avoid wasting time. Protect and enhance your future by making every moment work for you now.

Remember these tips to help you organize your time:

1. Define goals.
2. Set priorities.
3. Develop priority lists.
4. Make yourself a priority—schedule time to relax.
5. Keep your priorities realistic; let others help.
6. Follow your priority lists.
7. Keep time logs to help you reschedule better.
8. Review, evaluate, and revise your lists, calendars, and logs.
9. Make a backup plan to avoid letting crises upset your scheduling.
10. Use all your time—travel time, waiting time—for thinking out problems and jotting down ideas.

Questions to Ask Yourself

Effective scheduling can help you achieve your long-term goals. Remember that the future is not so far away. 1) What are your long-term goals? How do you plan to get from here to there? 2) What affects our actions more than any other factor? 3) What can you do to organize your time well?

Glossary

brainstorming Breaking down goals into smaller parts by listing ideas that pop freely into your mind.

budget To plan how resources such as money or time are used.

cluster To schedule similar tasks close to each other.

contingency planning Making backup or emergency plans in case something unexpected interferes with your scheduling.

deadline A time by which something must be done.

delegating Asking someone else to take responsibility for some of your tasks.

long-term goals Tasks you want to accomplish within a long period of time—a week, a month, or a year.

overcommit To take on more tasks than one has time for.

priority list List of tasks ranked in order of importance.

procrastinate To delay doing tasks; to put things off.

reevaluate To determine the value or effectiveness of something.

sequencing Planning a series of small steps leading to a larger goal.

short-term goals Tasks you want to accomplish within a short period of time—today, tomorrow, or in a few days.

time log A record of how time is spent.

For Further Reading

Arnold, John D. *Make Up Your Mind*. New York: AMACOM, 1978.

Gilbert, Sara. *Go For It: Get Organized*. New York: Morrow Junior Books, 1990.

James, Elizabeth, and Barkin, Carol. *How to Be School Smart: Secrets of Successful Schoolwork*. New York: Lothrop, Lee and Shepard, 1983.

Klein, David, and Klein, Mary Mae. *Yourself Ten Years From Now*. New York: Harcourt Brace Jovanovich, Inc., 1977.

Ross, Olney, and Walker, Patricia. *Time: How to Have More of It*. New York: Walker & Co., 1983.

Challenging Reading

Allen, Kathleen R., Ph.D. *Time and Information Management That Really Works*! Lincolnwood, IL: NTC Publishing Group, 1995.

Culp, Stephanie. *Streamlining Your Life*. Cincinnati: Writer's Digest Books, 1991.

Lee, Richard S., and Lee, Mary Price. *Coping Through Effective Time Management*. New York: The Rosen Publishing Group, 1991.

Index

About the Author

Sue Hurwitz earned an M.A. in Education at the University of Missouri. She has taught every grade K-9. She is the author of *Careers Inside the World of Government* and *Careers Inside the World of Entrepreneurs.* She is coauthor of *Sally Ride: Shooting for the Stars, Drugs and Your Friends, Hallucinogens, Drugs and Birth Defects, Staying Healthy, Applications: Filling Out All Kinds of Forms, Working Together Against Homelessness,* and *Coping with Homelessness.*

Photos

Cover by Kim Sonsky. All other photos by Matthew Baumann and Kim Sonsky.

Layout and Design

Kim Sonsky